A Daily Pilgrim Devotional

A Daily Pilgrim Devotional

G. M. T. BROSIUS

RESOURCE *Publications* · Eugene, Oregon

A DAILY PILGRIM DEVOTIONAL

The author wishes to express his gratitude to Harvard University Press, Princeton University Press, and HarperOne for their permission to cite previous important works and translations.

Resource Publications
An Imprint of Wipf and Stock Publishers
199 W. 8th Ave., Suite 3
Eugene, OR 97401

www.wipfandstock.com

PAPERBACK ISBN: 978-1-7252-8886-7
HARDCOVER ISBN: 978-1-7252-8887-4
EBOOK ISBN: 978-1-7252-8888-1

03/31/21

Follow on Instagram @adailypilgrimdevotional

To her, the one true supporter in all my endeavours,
holding my hand along the way of hope;
Charlotte Brosius.
To her mother, who in pain still found time to drive me
on the road of goodness; Marietta Campbell.
To the fair maiden; Sarah Best who was a friend no
matter which trail my steps led me.
And to Chris Lahowitch; she always a listener
while I journey life's toilsome paths to peace.

Preface

Basil the Great in the fourth century AD instructed many that to seek truth, was a lifelong mission. As such, during the next 35 days, may each devotion aid your *camino* in contemplation of that mission. There is not a direct path nor one direct journey which leads us. As we begin to walk, we are like a newly born fawn. Our legs wobbly as we are unsure where to step. We can not begin our path like an athlete who expects to be crowned gold. Yet, remain steadfast as time allows us to prepare our spirit in strength so by ascending difficult roads, we inevitably understand our purpose. Perhaps, your current path needs to be examined? In this, ancient philosophers, writers and theologians advised that we should adapt the 'branches of knowledge' as in the Doric proverb. In the prospect of life's journey, we should seek their truth and emanate them. Their lyrical hymns and words have left us with a safe passage to aid our soul in attainment of wisdom. Pilgrimaging always result in an unexpected transformation of our being.

> *Draw nigh o'er chapels, come hither this place*
> *awaits your presence, shrines erected, majestic*

mysteries reveal thy heart's anchor. Oh pilgrim!
Lo, fear forges thy shackles holding courage's step.

May your steps lead to your destiny however many paths necessary. Just keep walking! *Buen Camino*!

Before the Journey

"Be a lamp, or a lifeboat, or a ladder. Help someone's soul heal.
Walk out of your house like a shepherd . . . You have been a
source of pain. Now you will be the delight. . . You have been
an unsafe house. Now you will be the one who sees into the
invisible. . ."

—RUMI, *A Well-Baked Loaf*

Whatever road you have travelled, the pilgrim knows when
he or she has reached their destination. Along the way they
have suffered more from the heart than of the body. They
have healed their shortcomings, their regrets, their own
judgments and those against others. The pain of suffering
build stones, a foundation to weather Fate's battle.

Now, it is time to be a teacher, manifest the 'unknow-
able' to the throng thirsty for wisdom.

Memorializing
Before the Journey

{The day's Meditations & Prayers. The distance travelled, those we encountered on our path, places and sights that have left an imprint on our senses; all may be documented here.}

Day 1

For it is time for him to set upon his journey, carrying a heavy burden that love requires one to bear, he expels his soul with the concerns of the world so that his heart may be light and free over the rough and hard path.

Because long and perilous is the journey which I make in search of my Beloved, I must seek him with great faith and journey, with all speed. Fervour ignited his will, fear preserved him from danger bringing him to those moss-laden lands which brought him joy and humility in honour of whom he sought.

—RAMON LULL

Ramon Lull was determined to proclaim the Beloved's mystery to the impious. His journey was one of great hardship, destitution and failure. Cast out to fringes of medieval kingdoms, he finally met his beloved after heretics in the early fourteenth century stoned him to death in the ancient city of Bugia. He was martyred for his faith and his romantic mysticism now remains centuries later.

Memorializing Day 1

{The day's Meditations & Prayers. The distance travelled, those we encountered on our path, places and sights that have left an imprint on our senses; all may be documented here.}

Day 2

Therefore, it is not given to everyone to climb this road, rough at first and hard to travel and full of abundant sweat and toil, so steep it is, yet if one essays to climb it, the summit is easily to reach. But once he has ascended, he is able to see how smooth and more pleasant the travel. The task keeps man from cowardness and becoming weak which is more benign than the road to vice.

—BASIL THE GREAT

In the fourth century AD, Basil a renowned Christian philosopher was educated by the likes of Origen and Gregory of Nazianzus. He wrote a treatise *To Young Men, on How They Might Derive Profit From Greek Literature*. It is here he defends the pagan classics and references the ancient writer Hesiod.

The path of toil leads to a destination of greatness for one's soul. The summit ascent cannot be reached without it.

Memorializing Day 2

{The day's Meditations & Prayers. The distance travelled, those we encountered on our path, places and sights that have left an imprint on our senses; all may be documented here.}

Day 3

Happy are the people whose strength is in you! Whose hearts are set on the pilgrims' way.

—PSALM 84:4

In this Psalm, the pilgrim is rejoiced. He is celebrated for trusting in faith to persevere. Knowing the ground in which he walks is a foundation to prepare his soul homeward. Walking, the soul becomes virtuous and pious.

Amongst the timbers shading our journey from a contrite heart the poppies blind our sight; we must ply our soul to the newness of God. It desires to be near Gods court. The sounds of nature awaken our senses to his majesty. Mysteries unfold in our spirit to bestow wisdom in the knowledge of enduring love.

Memorializing Day 3

{The day's Meditations & Prayers. The distance travelled, those we encountered on our path, places and sights that have left an imprint on our senses; all may be documented here.}

Day 4

But the soul becomes more and more worth loving the longer
it progresses toward wisdom.

—Xenophon

We continue the journey so the soul's valour break habits of
pleasure and comfort. Stains of ignorance, spots of ingratitude and fears are admonished. The soul sunders yet within
rises to that lofty height where it, the soul, reveals its true
purpose to the body. The path leads like a pattern weaver
needling the thread.

To understand what was inconceivable, step-by-step
destiny reveals cognizance necessary in man's wisdom, to
neglect distractions hindering passions of our intelligent
soul over our primal body.

Memorializing Day 4

{The day's Meditations & Prayers. The distance travelled, those we encountered on our path, places and sights that have left an imprint on our senses; all may be documented here.}

Day 5

God ordains any of his children to pursue a path which does
not lead sooner or later to felicity and he never partakes from
the bosom of knowledge of the most secret mystery, where
wisdom is not suffocated by the vice of ingratitude.

—Hissman of Gottingen

As the moon wax and wanes, each day allows us to overcome grievances, pleasures vainly pursued 'till that day we
claim victory for virtue!

An oracle foretells that a soul will journey over the
rocky sea while fear prohibits ever leaving the harbour's
safety. A divine light gives peace to the human spirit so
that the unknown challenge is destiny's course to a greater
purpose.

Memorializing Day 5

{The day's Meditations & Prayers. The distance travelled,
those we encountered on our path, places and sights that
have left an imprint on our senses; all may be documented
here.}

Day 6

The more masters we capture, the more masters we will serve.

—SENECA

Diogenes the Cynic tells us that we shall periodically surrender pleasure and experience discomfort. The battle an individual undergoes with either victory or defeat over vice of pleasure is extraordinary.

Sleep on a hard floor, fast the evening meal, deprive the throat of water when it is dry, dress homily for a day, remove yourself in meditation—all acts are self-induced even though we have the remedy at hand will allow us as humans, appreciate more.

Instead of our desires casting us into a continuous realm of pride and gluttony; self-denial lightens the scale.

Memorializing Day 6

{The day's Meditations & Prayers. The distance travelled, those we encountered on our path, places and sights that have left an imprint on our senses; all may be documented here.}

Day 7

Camino a Santiago el peregrino aprende, entiende y vive;
ya su regreso, como testigo comparte lo que ha vivido, oido y
aprendido.

—Jose Fernandez Lago

As quoted by the Archbishop of Santiago de Compostela in 1999, pilgrimage has changed the pilgrim. A tourist becomes a pilgrim and receives many blessings from the journey. The many types of people walking begin in a multitude of conditions. They begin in every sort of condition. The poor ones become rich in spirit, those weak and malnourished become healthy, those whom have grievances, resentment and anger within their hearts find peace, those whom are debased and uncompassionate for their fellow humans become humble and sensitive, those with avarice and full of vice in greed and selfishness become generous and those who profess falsehoods and hypocrisy become fair and loyal servants to the truth. Those sad, now rejoice when tears have been dried.

May the *peregrino* be forever a witness to the profound power of the way of St. James.

Memorializing Day 7

{The day's Meditations & Prayers. The distance travelled, those we encountered on our path, places and sights that have left an imprint on our senses; all may be documented here.}

Day 8

Une thereapie par l'espace, le pelerinage demeure essentiellement depart.

—Alphonse Dupront

Dupront believed that pilgrimage is the act of leaving, "it is a therapy of distance."[1]

The tombs of the martyred saints were not accessible to everyone. Many were great distances from the faithful. It was this distance which would define a pilgrim. The pilgrim's journey would be that path where his desires could not be appeased locally. The commitment to travel the distance on foot, boat, or by beast of burden symbolizes his inner yearning to leave.

The distance provides him or her with an intimate closeness with the Divine. It was the distance that prepared the pilgrim with a therapeutic healing that so he or she would be closer to the *praesentia*.

Memorializing Day 8

{The day's Meditations & Prayers. The distance travelled, those we encountered on our path, places and sights that have left an imprint on our senses; all may be documented here.}

Day 9

Go into the chapel where you pray to the Lord. And what you will find there will be a consolation to you on your journey.

—GREGORY OF TOURS

How many have been healed by tears in prayer? Are tears a cleansing of vice which has taken residence within? Tears of 'supreme contrition' are but a way station for the pilgrim as a conduit to heaven's highway as said by Gregory of Tours. Standing or kneeling in prayer has the same benefit—the bowed head shows our submission of guilt, deeds requited and deeds done reluctantly.

Since the fourth century AD, the City of Tours hosts the remains of Bishop Martin. Pilgrims walk in faith and prostrate their shortcomings in fervent prayer. May St. Martin bless and heal you like one of the many pilgrims who beseeches him to perform miracles of centuries past.

Memorializing Day 9

{The day's Meditations & Prayers. The distance travelled, those we encountered on our path, places and sights that have left an imprint on our senses; all may be documented here.}

Day 10

"The soul comes every day at dawn. *Good to see you again my friend. The peace of God be with you.*"[2]

—RUMI

It is great to be alive. The sound of the cock knows light's early break. We feel youth. We begin anew like a caterpillar transforming into God's handiwork. In the depths of darkness, the still soul breaks for freedom.

In a world of despair, look for the one who will guide you on your way.

Memorializing Day 10

{The day's Meditations & Prayers. The distance travelled, those we encountered on our path, places and sights that have left an imprint on our senses; all may be documented here.}

Day 11

Tertullian in a treatise says that a Christian could expect to awake in a divine state after he or she had become a believer of the martyred saint.

The martyr prayer by Macrina, "*Place beside me an angel of light, to lead me by the hand so that the impious one does not stand against me on my way.*"[3]

A relationship with a martyred saint; allows an individual to have an intercessor acting on his or her behalf to guide him or her on an easier road to heaven rather than the straight, narrow path that most were unable to locate. An intercessor is a protector, a shield impervious from decay and vice, along ones journey. As friend to Christ; the martyr becomes a true servant of God.

Through a divine hand the individual can bridge the celestial with a dialogue of companionship and identity. The individual has a guardian for his or her soul and a direct connection to the holy.

Per conservum beneficia sumanus.

Memorializing Day 11

{The day's Meditations & Prayers. The distance travelled, those we encountered on our path, places and sights that have left an imprint on our senses; all may be documented here.}

Day 12

Oh, dear father, thou are surrounded by a dense mist of ignorance and walking in darkness, thou see not even one small glimmer of light. Thou have lost the right pathway and wander over terrible cliffs and chasms. Holding darkness for light, it sweetens and tickles at first, but time becomes sharper than a two-edged sword and more bitter than gall.

—ST. JOHN OF DAMASCENE

In the Byzantine Roman epic of *Barlaam & Iaosoph*, Ioasaph converts to Christianity and attempts to teach his father King Abenner, that if he continues to walk along a path of idolatry and make sacrifice to the Gods his soul will be eternally condemned. The King's answer is to tempt his son with all the riches of his empire. Yet, Ioasaph is not blinded by his father's offerings. The King further appoints oracles and seers to weaken his son's resolve. However, after great erudition even the seers understand Iasoph's journey is the right path.

At the eleventh hour the King's waxen soul melted, he partook the truth drinking from the cup of the most merciful and compassionate grace.

Memorializing Day 12

{The day's Meditations & Prayers. The distance travelled, those we encountered on our path, places and sights that have left an imprint on our senses; all may be documented here.}

Day 13

"... Arriving is what you are destined for. But do not hurry the journey at all. Better if it lasts for years, so you're old by the time you reach it, wealthy with all you've gained along the way ..., Wise as you have become ..., you'll have understood by then it's meaning."

—C.P. CAVAFY

The epic journey of Odysseus to his homeland was not with ease. The Ante-Nicene christian fathers used Homer as a metaphor in their philosophical and theological writings. It was a method which would allow the pagans to understand the allegory in scriptures.

Cavafy in his historical poem "Ithaka" writes in a lyrical metre, "... the ship cannot comprehend the meaning of destiny until it has left the shore. ..."[4]

Memorializing Day 13

{The day's Meditations & Prayers. The distance travelled, those we encountered on our path, places and sights that have left an imprint on our senses; all may be documented here.}

Day 14

Travelled in the true contrabandista, style we took everything both the rough and smooth as we found it mingling with all classes and conditions in a kind of vagabond companion-ship. Rambling over hill, dale, moor and mountain which the traveller often does. The landscape has long sweeping plains, destitute of trees ineffable silent, lonesome and great cultivated grains that sway in the wind before sown, then the ground appears sunburnt and naked. One may catch a glimpse of a small village encroached on a precipice with towers of embattlements, a vestige of time now forsaken. Simple features impress upon the soul's feeling of sublimity, like the vastness of the ocean. It all has a hypnotic power over the human mind. To experience this is the true way to travel in Spain.

—WASHINGTON IRVING

Irving records in 1829 his extensive travels during several months he spent in Spain, much of his journey transformed how foreigners would visualize Spain through the Great Enlightenment Tour. Irving's romanticized stories contrib-uted to his legacy in more than one country as a cultural historian.

Memorializing Day 14

{The day's Meditations & Prayers. The distance travelled, those we encountered on our path, places and sights that have left an imprint on our senses; all may be documented here.}

Day 15

The Israelites were not led by the way of Philistines, although it was nearer.

—Exodus 13:17

Born in the twelfth century in Cordoba, Spain under the Almoravid dynasty, Maimonides was a philosopher, known for his study and extensive research on religious laws and medicine. Influenced by Sufism, he would be forced to convert to Islam from Judaism in order to survive. He believed that God chose the Israelites to walk not in the shortest distance but through the path which would prepare their souls in stages.

Human's habits are relinquished only through hardship. At each stage, a habit begins to loosen its grip and by walking the shorter route, the Israelites would not have prepared for what was to come. A walk in the light of redemption is only acquired through assiduousness over horn and wild rather through lea and steppe.

A pilgrimage to Cordoba enriches one's knowledge and increases thy wisdom at the birthplace of four great philosophers of antiquity: Seneca, Averroes, Avicenna and Maimonides.

Memorializing Day 15

{The day's Meditations & Prayers. The distance travelled, those we encountered on our path, places and sights that have left an imprint on our senses; all may be documented here.}

Day 16

We should not like sheep, follow the lead of the throng in front of us, travelling, thus the way that all go and not the way we ought to go.

—SENECA

A Stoic philosopher, Seneca often wrote to his eldest brother Gallio, a Roman official who held jurisdiction in Corinth. The Jews pleaded with Gallio to hold apostle Paul in condemnation of their faith. Could Gallio been influenced by the Stoic wisdom of his brother by not answering the Jews pleas?

Seneca's letter *On the Happy Life* teaches us that we must live based on reason, not on commonality. Our light should not be a lamp lit by another.

A pilgrimage to ancient Corinth would allow the pilgrim to stand on the marble platform where Paul appeared to Gallio to plead his innocence. Your journey will be long remembered.

Memorializing Day 16

{The day's Meditations & Prayers. The distance travelled, those we encountered on our path, places and sights that have left an imprint on our senses; all may be documented here.}

Day 17

Every pilgrim's journey is one of hope: the hope of reaching a destination successfully with the more profound hope that one's life will be bettered by that experience.

—CHRIS LOWNEY

In the book by Chris Lowney *A vanished world: Muslims, Christians and Jews in Medieval Spain*, Chris' historical writing on Spain's history and that of the great pilgrimage we call the Camino de Santiago explains that for thousands of years, humans of all faiths have bettered society for their pilgrimages.

The pilgrimage cleanses us with newness of purpose. As the pilgrim prayer states, "If from today, I don't continue walking your path searching and living according to what I have learned; in from today I do not see in every person, friend or foe a companion on the Camino; if from today I cannot recognize God, the father, the father of Jesus of Nazareth as the one God of my life I have arrived nowhere."[5]

Memorializing Day 17

{The day's Meditations & Prayers. The distance travelled, those we encountered on our path, places and sights that have left an imprint on our senses; all may be documented here.}

Day 18

The better road is the one toward what is just. Misery comes in abundance and is always nearby: Her road is smooth and is easy to achieve. But in front of excellence, God has set sweat and ache; Her path is long, steep and rough at first. Yet when one arrives at the top, it becomes easy, however the fool of misery blinds one by the simple path, without wisdom until the journey is completed. Excellence becomes easy only after conquering the difficulty.

—Hesiod

Known as the shepherd of verse, Hesiod in the seventh century BC proclaimed his writing was a result of a dream apparition. The treatise *Works & Days* imprinted in man's mind that he needs a map to lead him to resourcefulness and justice so that it may influence others to practice just acts.

> *Fortune favours valour o'er fear*
> *pain severs a chord of comfort.*
> *Will thy come partake the gifts*
> *midst the soul; Moab is waiting.*
> *Pourest thy full heart,*
> *stars will show thy way.*

Memorializing Day 18

{The day's Meditations & Prayers. The distance travelled, those we encountered on our path, places and sights that have left an imprint on our senses; all may be documented here.}

Day 19

Hic Locus est.

Here is the place.[6]

The long journey of the pilgrimage did not end at the entry point of the city or the village of the martyr. The pilgrim did not want to just follow the path to the tomb. He believed he was going to the place where he would see God's light, not just stare at decayed bones. Nearness to his light, was the pilgrim's hope of reward. He prayed that his feet would not fail him on his journey.

A way to prepare the devoted, the entry to the final resting place became a symbolism of the journey itself. In Tebessa, the shrine to the martyred St. Crispina would be juxtaposed with a high wall, great triumphal arches and long arcaded courtyards of 150 meters on the 'pilgrim's way' to prepare their final steps.

Salvum me fac.

Memorializing Day 19

{The day's Meditations & Prayers. The distance travelled, those we encountered on our path, places and sights that have left an imprint on our senses; all may be documented here.}

Day 20

The majestic city disgorges her Romans in a stream; with equal ardour patricians and the plebeian host are jumbled together, shoulder to shoulder for the faith banishes distinction of class.

—PRUDENTIUS

In his treatise *Peristephanon*, Prudentius writes about experiences of the throng of pilgrims that meander through the Holy City to the shrine of St. Hippolytus.

His observations were that you could not identify them by rank only by their devotion. Women and the poor previously unknown were uplifted in equality during their journey. It was while acting as a pilgrim man and woman were finally equal. Each sought a relationship with the Divine. It was through the act of pilgrimage communities were united. A melting pot of the new humanity, palaces and villages, fortresses, and farmlands. It is in the worship of Saints that Christianity became a religion, adapted from the worship of Gods and heroes of antiquity.

Memorializing Day 20

{The day's Meditations & Prayers. The distance travelled, those we encountered on our path, places and sights that have left an imprint on our senses; all may be documented here.}

Day 21

Two travellers on the road, both young and in good health, will differ in pace so that one will cover 200 stades to the other's 100. The former does what he has set out to do, by pressing ahead, while the other is in an easy-going mood, now resting by a fountain or in the shade, now gazing at the view, now looking for soft breezes.

— XENOPHON

One completes his course in record time, the other is delayed. But if each has the same destination, yet have different purposes shall one be more favourably? The fleet-footed, looks to the finish without contemplating the path which he journeyed. The laggard looks not in nearness but how he or she may receive blessings as traversing.

One is blinded by focus while the other is blinded by visions. As Theognis once said "Many imagined joy's they've never known, while few have seen joys only, they can know."

Memorializing Day 21

{The day's Meditations & Prayers. The distance travelled, those we encountered on our path, places and sights that have left an imprint on our senses; all may be documented here.}

Day 22

If the traveller following his star across the mountain becomes too absorbed in pondering ways of reaching the top, he risks forgetting which star shines the brightest for him. If we act merely for the sake of action, we will get nowhere. The pew attendant in the cathedral, overzealous about the annoyance of chairs risks forgetting that she serves a God. By absorbing myself in party politics, I risk forgetting that politics are meaningless unless they have a spiritual truth. I may dispute in favour of my chosen road, the road that another has taken. But I must respect the man, the spiritual being, if he toils towards the same star.

— Antoine de Saint Exupéry

In Antoine's famous novel *The Little Prince*, the challenges one may encounter may be different for man or woman. Fate's reason unbeknownst has purpose even when others have either more or less barriers to overcome.

It is providence that leads each to his or her guiding star wherever it may lead. We must respect each other even if the road is different than ours.

Memorializing Day 22

{The day's Meditations & Prayers. The distance travelled, those we encountered on our path, places and sights that have left an imprint on our senses; all may be documented here.}

Day 23

I then walked with more serene steps in search of some sequestered spot in the forest, some lonely place where no traces of human hands are evident, a retreat where no-one would intervene between nature and myself.

—ROUSSEAU

Do we also want to follow in the footsteps of Rousseau?

> When such societal ills are afflicting thy peace and passions are rife,
> Discover a secluded place that will kin' imagination, as
> the north wind brings a zest of self-sustenance in the sight, of a songbird with feathers celestial root, seemingly rouse the senses;
> Thy soul dullen by a gluttonous appetite longs to breath.

And he said, "Oh, that I had wings like a dove I would fly away, I would flee to a far-off place and make my lodging in the wilderness" (Psalm 55:7–8).

Memorializing Day 23

{The day's Meditations & Prayers. The distance travelled, those we encountered on our path, places and sights that have left an imprint on our senses; all may be documented here.}

Day 24

But how shall we find the way? What method can we devise? How can we see such inconceivable beauty? We cannot get there on foot, for our feet only carry us everywhere in this world, from one country to another. You must not get ready a carriage or a boat. Shut your eyes and let go in a way that everyone has but few uses. Let us fly on our journey, to the place where there are no shadows, to a place that is our soul's home.

—PLOTINUS

Plotinus so encapsulates a soul's journey in his Ennead *On Beauty*. In the third century AD, the great St. Augustine was inspired greatly by this Ennead that he references it in his famous *Confessions* to God.

Both men understood the journey each must take. The beauty of *courage* leads a bridle from fear's oppression and death. The beauty of *intellect* shields our mind from earthly to celestial. The beauty of *love* discovers true passions; find it, uncontaminated splendour not visible, a brilliant gaze, not the burning star, the self emanates the eyes to likeness of virtue.

Memorializing Day 24

{The day's Meditations & Prayers. The distance travelled, those we encountered on our path, places and sights that have left an imprint on our senses; all may be documented here.}

Day 25

When swept from its channel, life scatters in innumerable streams. It is difficult to foresee which route it will take in its treacherous and winding course. Today it flows in shallows like a rivulet over sand banks, so shallow that the shoals are visible, tomorrow it will flow richly and fully.

—MIKHAIL SHOLOKHOV

In *And Quiet Flows the Don* the author, Mikhail, writes a story about his heritage as a Cossack. The story comes to us with a meaning that life continues, although we do not know the outcome.

Fert, Fert, Fert!

Face today with the knowledge that the sense of neglect and wantonness will subside as the morning dew brings bounty not visible yester' morn'. It is with wisdom that life unabates along the ebbs and flows each day.

Memorializing Day 25

{The day's Meditations & Prayers. The distance travelled, those we encountered on our path, places and sights that have left an imprint on our senses; all may be documented here.}

Day 26

The distant and melancholy chime of the bell of some sequestered convent, the silence of universal nature in a tranquil night, the pure air we breathe on the summit of a lofty mountain, the canopy of the towering mystical forest, the ruined monuments of antiquity fill the soul with a soft melody and makes us forget the world and mankind.

—GEORGE ZIMMERMAN

Solitude was advantageous to many during the upheaval of revolutionary Europe. Zimmerman in the early nineteenth century corresponded with Catherine the Great of Russia. As an admirer of Zimmerman's philosophy and writings, Catherine sought to bring him to St. Petersburg as a member of her court but he graciously declined.

Through solitude, we become impervious to man's whim and his mischievous manipulations that do not but distract our soul from providence.

A soul longs for peace, yet you look in a place where it does not reside. You neglect to look within the cave of your being. How can that be found if you are not secluded?

Memorializing Day 26

{The day's Meditations & Prayers. The distance travelled, those we encountered on our path, places and sights that have left an imprint on our senses; all may be documented here.}

Day 27

The pilgrimage is a rite of introspection. It is the point that
you begin to look further and further inward so that even if
the path leads south or west, you feel as if your feet have taken
you in the depth of a country's soul. It is there you imagine
you discover a newness that has lied hidden for only your soul,
however widely your feet may take you.

—CEES NOOTEBOOM

In his extensive exploration of Spain, villages now long
expired and cities unrecognizable, Nooteboom documents
his experience in an insightful way. For those interested in
reaching the Valle de Silencio or the Shrine of Pelayo or
hear the cathedral bells ring out to their ears, each pilgrimage is a holy discovery of being.

Memorializing Day 27

{The day's Meditations & Prayers. The distance travelled, those we encountered on our path, places and sights that have left an imprint on our senses; all may be documented here.}

Day 28

"All day I think about it, then at night I say it. Where did I come from, and what am I supposed to be doing? I do not know. My soul is from elsewhere. I am sure of that and I intend to end up there."

— RUMI[7]

It is man's perpetual question. Fate procures understanding after thy soul discovers destiny's path.

We are curious creatures, born in a womb, man and beast are begotten to contemplate and to act in a manner which befits him. Many waste the time allotted, spinning to and fro purposeless. The scythe cuts the kernel at harvest not in sand but fertile plain. Man ordained to master beast, yet both born to serve. The populace chooses rule with sound vice, clambering all to the yoke hiding the foundation of the pure path leading to beauty and good.

Memorializing Day 28

{The day's Meditations & Prayers. The distance travelled, those we encountered on our path, places and sights that have left an imprint on our senses; all may be documented here.}

Day 29

I want only to bring you along the paths in which I have preceded you. Let you swim in the sea I have just crossed, so that it will bear you as it did me, under gone the same experience so that your eyes see with the eyes of your soul all that I have seen.

—IBN TUFAYL

He would have known of the pilgrimage to Santiago just like the pilgrimage to Jerusalem and to Mecca. A philosophical tale written by Ibn Tufayl in the twelfth century, is a religious story where the main character Hayy is born in solitude, nurtured by animals. Throughout the story, Hayy devotes his life in full contemplation on man's being. He asks, "How can a soul find attainment?"[8]

The proverb speaks to all pilgrims who begin to search for answers that remain unrevealed until they reach their destination.

Memorializing Day 29

{The day's Meditations & Prayers. The distance travelled, those we encountered on our path, places and sights that have left an imprint on our senses; all may be documented here.}

Day 30

Come, I will dry thy tears; I will inspire the wounded heart with courage; I will attend thee and sympathize in all thy afflictions; I will assist thee to support them; I will forge thy sorrows, awaken the senses to the divine nature and direct the sight to that God who is merciful who strews our path with flowers.

—Madame von Doring

In consolation to a devoted friend, grief of a loved one can be tremendous. We as humans lose much throughout our lives. Each day we say good-bye to those we saw only once and to those we cherish we watch take a final bow. We say *adieu* to each achievement and excitedly desire a new one to accomplish, we pass each challenge in triumph, and forget Fate's unending lesson.

Death is inevitable to our fleshly body. For youth's promise slips away, as a hare caught with holes in a net and the body's beauty dries; like the sculptor's chisel oxidizes in his frail hands (Job:14:1–2). Fortitude avails to lift us from slumber each day blest by a ready intercessor whose there to assist us in our way.

Memorializing Day 30

{The day's Meditations & Prayers. The distance travelled, those we encountered on our path, places and sights that have left an imprint on our senses; all may be documented here.}

Day 31

Men walk almost always in the path trodden by others, pro-
ceeding in their actions by imitation. Although he cannot take
the exact path, nor attain the same virtue of those he emulates,
a prudent man which observes greatness has duplicity in
inspiration to mirror his own.

—NICCOLÒ MACHIAVELLI

Machiavelli, a much mis-understood Renaissance Floren-
tine, wrote extensively about the ability to achieve one's
own potential. Niccolò's eternal slumber is reposed at the
gothic church of Sante Croce in Florence. The stele of his
legacy remains near the greatness of such individuals of
Michelangelo, Burni and Galileo.

A pilgrimage to Florence to see the final resting places
of some of the greatest Renaissance philosophers, states-
men and theologians humbles even the most modern pilgrim who dreams that his journey will end with a greatness
that matches his predecessors.

Memorializing Day 31

{The day's Meditations & Prayers. The distance travelled, those we encountered on our path, places and sights that have left an imprint on our senses; all may be documented here.}

Day 32

Oh! Allysus a fine maiden martyred, suffered under the flame,
valor Sebastian who took not one nor two nor three of the pointed shard,
the Apostle who left the pagan Isthmus by a Stoic brother's act,
either Isaac or Eulogic convicted of truth revealing,
Decius cut ten with his scythe under the Cretan sun and stained the earth,
the mass of pilgrims who walk the path, like the star beaming
guiding The Magi; to the remains, of these whom shall receive a humnos worthy?

In time may the mysteries be understood when our mind is capable. Let our feet rest at the temple of virtue; the journey to the hill of faith is lifelong. By forging our brethren's mind in compassion and justice, his or her hands will be moulded with Truth.

Memorializing Day 32

{The day's Meditations & Prayers. The distance travelled, those we encountered on our path, places and sights that have left an imprint on our senses; all may be documented here.}

Day 33

For I am a wanderer, fearful, bewildered, labouring, un-guided, failing, ignorant of this place, exhausted by my journey. Having striven to pass beyond, the spheres and enter the supernal realms, now, I totter and wonder alone, uncertain of the way, I seek to enter the sanctuary of God. The chamber of the Thunderer, to know the wisdom of the mysteries and the hidden pathways to heaven.

—ALAN OF LILLE

Alan wrote *Anti-Cladudianus*, in the twelfth century and was influenced by Prudentius and a fourth century AD, Claudian poet. Dante was inspired by Alan's work and it influenced his writing *Paradisio*.

Theology, in metaphor, tries to find her way from the terrestrial earth, her habitation, to the celestial stars, man's final destiny. She along with Providence, leads man on a journey of uncertainty. An epiphany uncovers man's spirit to a path of stirring tumultuousness. Some are ignorant as they are 'ill-suited' in their steps. Truth leads those to wisdom along the passageways.

We supplicate you, our healer, keep thy feet well and grant thy soul a beginning which reaches that lofty palace thereby gaining a labourer's reward.

Memorializing Day 33

{The day's Meditations & Prayers. The distance travelled, those we encountered on our path, places and sights that have left an imprint on our senses; all may be documented here.}

Day 34

Our lady of Remedies, Chalma, Compostela, Our lady of
Guadalupe, Le Puy, Lourdes, Lough Derg, Canterbury, Santa
Maria Maggiore, Loreto, Thessaloniki, Mt. Athos, Mar Saba,
Pharan, Mar Gabriel, Deir-al-Zaferan, Jerusalem, Mt. Sinai,
Deir-ul-Muharraq, Zuiho-in, The Henro.

Mother, Oh Holy! where shall you bear on
vast desert to burn thy skin so tender
taste lone gall while infante waits for shelter,
tyrant heels approach, the sword is thirsty.
Now his life is spared by formless unchanging.
Take the rein and lead 'em principled one.
Though place providence has ruled will serve as flare
time anew, will feet to toil there.

Memorializing Day 34

{The day's Meditations & Prayers. The distance travelled, those we encountered on our path, places and sights that have left an imprint on our senses; all may be documented here.}

After the Journey

The long straight line of the highway, distant town that seems
so near, the peasants in the fields, that stay their toil to cross
themselves and pray, when from the belfry at midday the
angles they hear; white hamlets in fields of wheat, while cities
slumbering by the sea, white sunshine flooding square and
street, dark mountain ranges, at whose feet the river bends are
dry with heat-all was a dream to me.

—Henry Wadsworth Longfellow

In the late nineteenth century, Longfellow set out to com-
prise a voluminous collection of prose on all the great places
one could travel. It is in Spain, where he penned this as part
of the many writings he collected while traveling in Europe.
We dream and imagine. In our imagination we never per-
ceive that it to be true nor the experience to become a part
of our Fate. However, sometimes the reality of a dream is
better than the imagination.

Memorializing the
After the Journey

{The day's Meditations & Prayers. The distance travelled, those we encountered on our path, places and sights that have left an imprint on our senses; all may be documented here.}

Additional thoughts and experiences to be memorialized

Additional thoughts and experiences to be memorialized

Additional thoughts and experiences to be memorialized

Additional thoughts and experiences to be memorialized

Endnotes

1. Brown, *Cult of the Saints*, 88.
2. Moyne, Rumi: The Big Red Book, "A World Dense with Greeting"
3. Brown, *Cult of the Saints*, 66–67.
4. Cavafy, *Poets' Voice*, 8–9.
5. Prayer card; Santa Maria La Real, O'Cebreiro, Spain.
6. Brown, *Cult of the Saints*, 86.
7. Moyne, Rumi: The Big Red Book, "Who Says Words with my Mouth"
8. Paraphrase of Tufayl et al., *Hayy Ibn Yaqzan*, 7.

Bibliography

Alan of Lille. *Literary Works*. Edited and translated by Winthrop Wetherbee. DOML 22. Cambridge, MA: Harvard University Press, 2013.

Basil. *Letters Vol. IV: 249–368; On Greek Literature*. Translated by Roy J. Deferrari. First published 1934. LCL 270. Cambridge, MA: Harvard University Press, 1934.

Brown, Peter. *The Cult of the Saints*. Chicago: University of Chicago Press, 2015.

Cavafy, C. P. *The Poets' Voice*. Excerpted from "Ithaka," Collected Poems. Translated by Edmund Keeley and Philip Sherrard, edited by George Savidis. Rev. ed. Translation copyright 1975, 1992 by Edmund Keely and Philip Sherrard. Reprinted by permission of Princeton University Press. Athens: Hellenic Parliament Foundation for Parliamentarism and Democracy, 2013.

Gerber, Douglas E., ed. and trans. *Greek Elegiac Poetry: From the Seventh to the Fifth Centuries BC*. LCL 258. Cambridge, MA: Harvard University Press, 1999.

Gregory of Tours. *Lives and Miracles*. Edited and translated by Giselle de Nie. DOML 39. Cambridge, MA: Harvard University Press, 2015.

Hesiod. *Theogony, Works and Days, Testimonia*. Translated by Glenn W. Most. LCL 57. Cambridge MA: Harvard University Press, 2006.

Irving, Washington. *Tales of the Alhambra*. Granada, Spain: Ediciones Miguel Sanchez. 1832.

John Damascene. *Barlaam and Ioasaph*. Translated by G. R. Woodward et al. LCL 34. Cambridge, MA: Harvard University Press, 1967.

Lago, Fernandez Jose. *Apostle of Saint James Life, Death and Burial*. Translated by Juan Jose Varela et al. 6th ed. Graficas Lopa, 2009.

Lowney, Chris. *A Vanished World: Muslims, Christians, and Jews in Medieval Spain*. Oxford: Oxford University Press, 2006.

Lull, Ramon. *The Book of the Lover and the Beloved*. Translated by E. Allison Peers. Whitefish, MT: Kessinger Reprints, 2010.

Machiavelli, Niccolò. *The Prince*. Translated by Luigi Ricci, revised by E. R. P. Vincent.

Moyne, John, et al. "A Well-Baked Loaf." In *Rumi: The Big Red Book*, 295. Collected translations by Coleman Barks. San Francisco: HarperOne, 2011.

———. "Who Says Words with My Mouth?" In *Rumi: The Big Red Book*, 352. Collected translations by Coleman Barks. HarperOne, 2011.

———. "A World Dense with Greeting." In *Rumi: The Big Red Book*, 287. Collected translations by Coleman Barks. San Francisco: HarperOne, 2011.

Nooteboom, Cees. *Roads to Santiago*. New York: Vintage, 2014.

Plotinus. *Porphyry on the Life of Plotinus, Ennead I*. Vol. I. Translated by A. H. Armstrong. LCL 440. Cambridge MA: Harvard University Press, 1966.

Saint-Exupery, Antoine de. *The Little Prince*. London: Penguin, 1995.

Seneca. *Moral Essays Vol. II*. Translated by John W. Basore. First published 1932. LCL 254. Cambridge, MA: Harvard University Press, 1932.

Sholokhov, Mikhail. *And Quiet Flows the Don*. Translated by Stephen Garry. New York: Penguin Random House, 2016.

Stroumsa, Sarah. *Maimonides in His World*. Princeton: Princeton University Press, 2011.

Tufayl, Ibn, et al. *Hayy Ibn Yaqzan: A Philosophical Tale*. Translated by Lenn Evan Goodman. Chicago: University of Chicago Press, 2009.

Xenophon. *Memorabilia, Oeconomicus, Symposium, Apology*. Translated by E. C. Marchant et al., Revised by Jeffrey Henderson. LCL 168. Cambridge, MA: Harvard University Press, 2013.

Zimmerman, George John. *An Examination on the Advantages of Solitude Vols. I & II*. London: James Cundee, 1809.